His feet are webbed to help support him on soft mud.

American flamingos have pink and gray feet.

# Fabulous Floyd

## The True Story of a Flamingo Who Never Gave Up
### by Georgeanne Irvine

Published by SAN DIEGO ZOO GLOBAL PRESS

*Fabulous Floyd: The True Story of a Flamingo Who Never Gave Up* was published by San Diego Zoo Global Press in association with Blue Sneaker Press. Through these publishing efforts, we seek to inspire multiple generations to care about wildlife, the natural world, and conservation.

San Diego Zoo Global is committed to leading the fight against extinction. It saves species worldwide by uniting its expertise in animal care and conservation science with its dedication to inspire a passion for nature.

Douglas G. Myers, President and Chief Executive Officer
Shawn Dixon, Chief Operating Officer
Yvonne Miles, Corporate Director of Retail
Georgeanne Irvine, Director of Corporate Publishing
San Diego Zoo Global
P.O. Box 120551
San Diego, CA 92112-0551
sandiegozoo.org  |  619-231-1515

San Diego Zoo Global's publishing partner is Blue Sneaker Press, an imprint of Southwestern Publishing Group, Inc., 2451 Atrium Way, Nashville, TN 37214. Southwestern Publishing Group is a wholly owned subsidiary of Southwestern/Great American, Inc., Nashville, Tennessee.

Christopher G. Capen, President, Southwestern Publishing Group
Carrie Hasler, Development Director, Blue Sneaker Press
Kristin Connelly, Managing Editor
Lori Sandstrom, Art Director/Graphic Designer
swpublishinggroup.com | 800-358-0560

ISBN: 978-1-943198-05-4
Library of Congress Control Number: 2018930225
Printed in China
10 9 8 7 6 5 4 3 2 1

To fabulous Floyd and his flock,
who inspire people every day to love flamingos, and to his
human caretakers and friends, who never gave up on him!

## Acknowledgments:

### MY SINCEREST APPRECIATION TO THE FOLLOWING PEOPLE FOR HELPING ME SHARE FLOYD'S STORY WITH CHILDREN EVERYWHERE:

Kristina Nelson; Krista Perry; Christine Molter, DVM; Kathy Marmack; Kelly Elkins; Beth Bicknese, DVM; Nicole LaGreco; Athena Wilson; Heidi Bernard; Charmaine Davis; Lorena Walton; Maureen Duryee; Wendy Ricker; Hannah Ellis; Susan Patch; Mark Freeland; Marielle Santiago; Janet Hawes; Meredith Reid; Christina Kaullen; Lori Sandstrom; Carrie Hasler; Lisa Bissi; Jen MacEwen; Ken Bohn; Mary Sekulovich; Yvonne Miles; Diane Cappelletti; Angel Chambosse; Victoria Garrison; Debra Erickson; Dave Rimlinger; Geoff Pye, DVM; Karen Kearns, DVM; Joshua Jackson, DVM; Gary Priest; Shawn Dixon; Douglas Myers; Chris Capen; Peggy Blessing; Judi Myers; Andrea, Savannah, and Elijah Cletus; Tara, Ashlynn, and Corben Saylor; Nomsa and Logan Burkhardt; and Aaron, Hudson, and Weston Perry.

### PHOTO CREDITS
**Ken Bohn:** 4, 6, 7, 8, 10, 11, 15 left, 16 left, 17 top, 23, 24, 25 top, 27 right, 28, 29, 30, 31, 33 bottom, back cover.
**Christine Molter, DVM:** 14 left, 15 right, 16 right, 17 bottom, 18, 20, 21, 22, 26 top left.
**Georgeanne Irvine:** front cover, title page 1, 3, 12, 13 center, 19, 32, 33 top.
**Christina Kaullen:** 9, 14 right. **Meredith Reid:** 26 right top and bottom. **Kristina Nelson:** 27 bottom left.
**Lori Sandstrom:** 5. **Kathy Marmack:** 25 left. **Shutterstock:** 13 right, 34 top and right, 35, 36.
**Alejandro Prieto/Biosphoto/Minden Pictures:** 34 lower left. **Krista Perry:** back jacket flap.

# It Started with an Egg

Floyd is the friendliest flamingo at the San Diego Zoo. His life began in an egg, laid by his mother on a tall mud nest.

Flamingos live in lagoons, mangrove swamps, and large, shallow lakes. They can live in salt or fresh water.

Visitors feed the flamingos a special treat from a cup: dog kibble mixed with water.

Even before he hatched, keepers knew Floyd's life would be different. He was destined to have a special job at the Zoo. When Floyd grew up, he would join a flock of friendly flamingos that had been trained to like people. These flamingos, called animal ambassadors, let people meet and feed them while animal trainers explain why flamingos are so amazing.

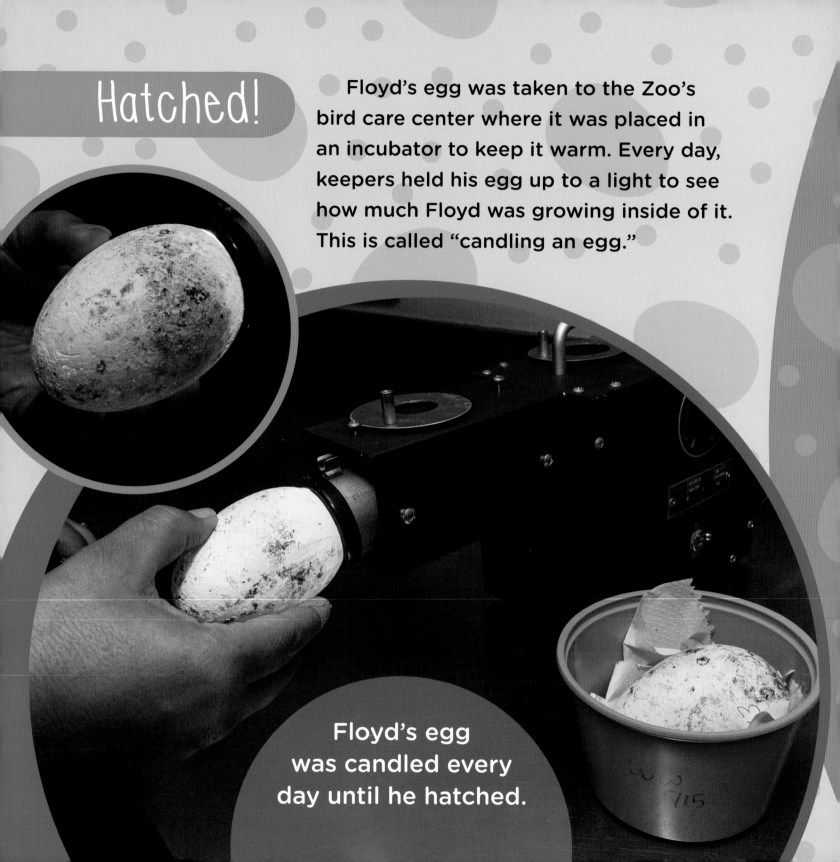

# Hatched!

Floyd's egg was taken to the Zoo's bird care center where it was placed in an incubator to keep it warm. Every day, keepers held his egg up to a light to see how much Floyd was growing inside of it. This is called "candling an egg."

Floyd's egg was candled every day until he hatched.

After 30 days, Floyd hatched by breaking through his thick eggshell with his beak. He looked like a little gray fuzzball with legs! A few other flamingo chicks hatched at the same time as Floyd, so the keepers painted a different-colored spot on each chick to tell them apart. Floyd's spot was green.

Animal trainers, who were in charge of the friendly flamingos, took the chicks on daily walks to exercise them. This also helped the chicks bond with people.

After a walk, the trainers sat on the ground with the baby flamingos. Floyd was special and different from the very start. He always climbed into someone's lap and snuggled up to that person. If the other chicks were blocking his way into a lap, he pushed them away. They liked people, but not as much as Floyd did!

When the chicks heard the trainers' voices, they came running, because they liked being with them.

Introducing Floyd!

When Floyd was three months old, he and the other chicks were introduced to the flock of grown-up friendly flamingos in the Zoo. At first, the adult flamingos didn't pay much attention to the young birds, but soon they were buddies.

As Floyd grew taller, he began having trouble standing up straight, which concerned the trainers. Flamingos need to have two strong, sturdy legs to survive! They must be able to walk with their flock and wade in the water to eat. They also need to be able to stand on one leg, so they can rest the other one.

# Two Left Feet?

The trainers noticed that something was wrong with Floyd's right leg. It was crooked, and his right foot pointed in the same direction as the left one. It looked like Floyd had two left feet!

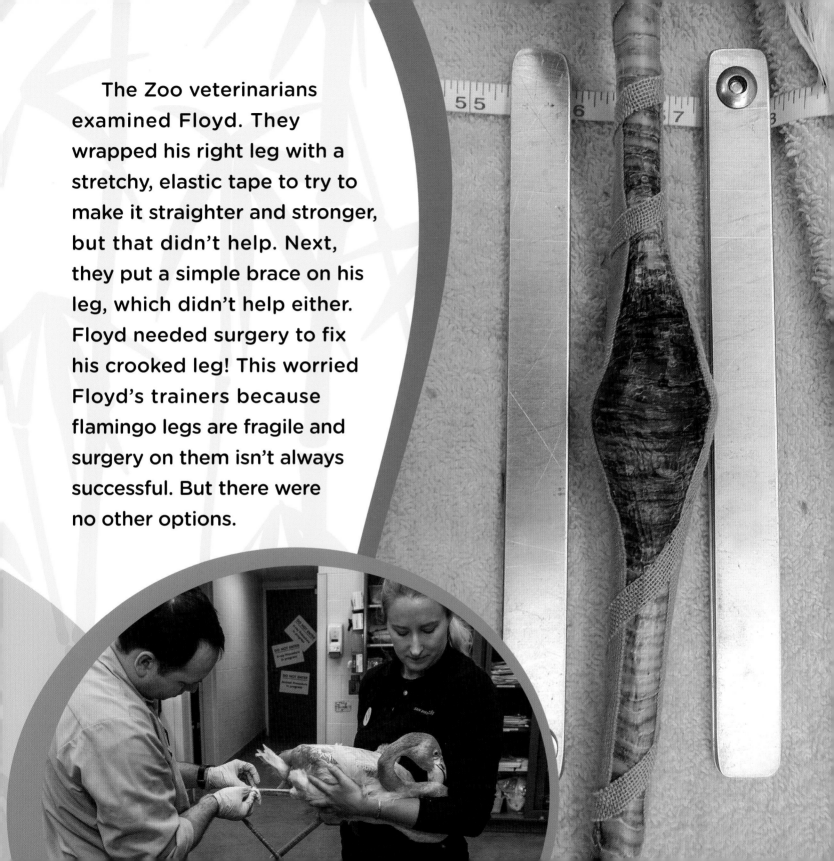

The Zoo veterinarians examined Floyd. They wrapped his right leg with a stretchy, elastic tape to try to make it straighter and stronger, but that didn't help. Next, they put a simple brace on his leg, which didn't help either. Floyd needed surgery to fix his crooked leg! This worried Floyd's trainers because flamingo legs are fragile and surgery on them isn't always successful. But there were no other options.

# Floyd's Surgery

The morning of the surgery, Floyd snuggled in the lap of a trainer while they were driven to the Zoo hospital in a small truck. At the hospital, Floyd was given medicine to make him go to sleep. A clear mask was put over Floyd's beak to help him breathe and stay asleep during the operation.

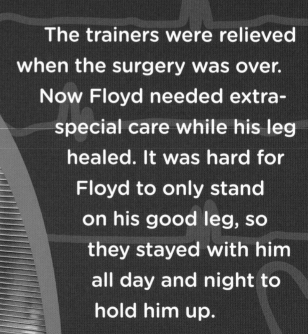

The trainers were relieved when the surgery was over. Now Floyd needed extra-special care while his leg healed. It was hard for Floyd to only stand on his good leg, so they stayed with him all day and night to hold him up.

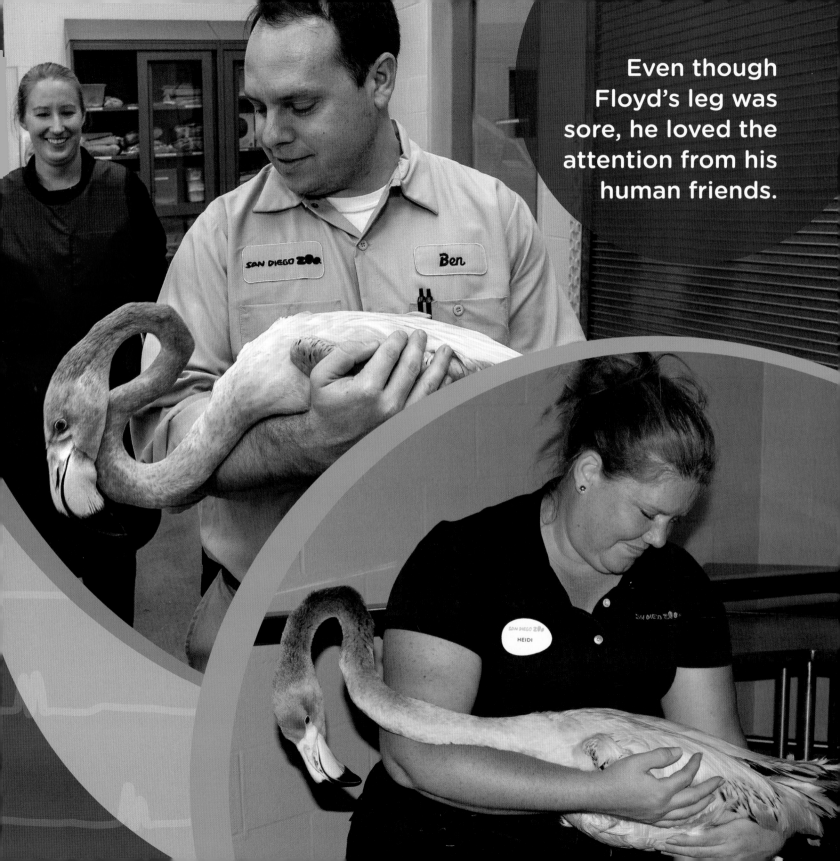

Even though Floyd's leg was sore, he loved the attention from his human friends.

But then after the surgery Floyd's foot unexpectedly began to swell. His trainers waded into a small pool with him, so he could soak his foot in water to help it heal. His leg bandage was always wrapped in a plastic bag—it wasn't supposed to get wet. As Floyd got stronger, the trainers filled the pool with more water to make it deeper. That way, Floyd could easily dunk his head as well as wash and preen his feathers, which are everyday flamingo behaviors.

The trainers were overjoyed when Floyd's right leg and foot finally healed. Now he was able to join the other flamingos again.

They could tell he was glad to be back with the flock because he honked, stomped around, and flapped his wings!

SD133681
SAN DIEGO ZOO, FLOYD
M
012M

3D VR

09-Sep
Acq: 10:12:09.714677
Se: 557-5/5
Im: 1/40

8.86 cm

167.8°

VSHSDCT
OsiriX
VETERINARY SPECIALTY HO...
DFOV: 35.5 x 50.3 cm

SD133681
SAN DIEGO ZOO, FLOYD
M
012M

H

09-Sep
Acq: 10:02:33.12
Se:
Im:
Loc: A174

R

L

11038.00 ms
0°
20 mA
110 kV
T20s
Thk: 1.0 mm
Zoom: 1.19x
W:500 L:50 (WIN

## Bad News

Soon after rejoining the flock, the trainers
received bad news from the veterinarians. Floyd
also needed surgery on his left leg because it
had grown crooked, too.

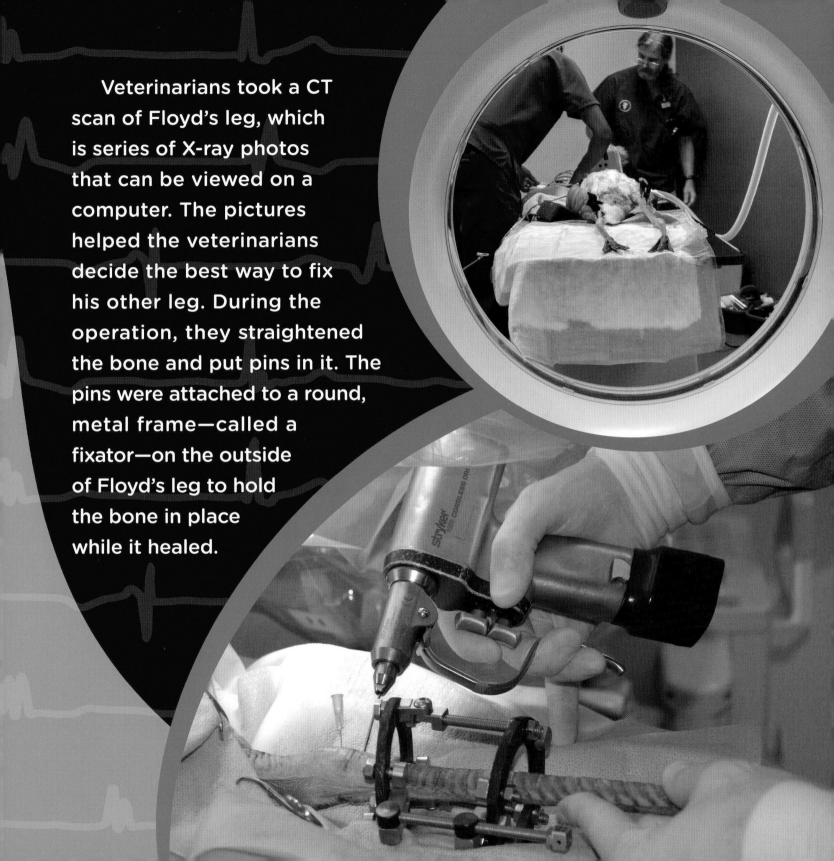

Veterinarians took a CT scan of Floyd's leg, which is series of X-ray photos that can be viewed on a computer. The pictures helped the veterinarians decide the best way to fix his other leg. During the operation, they straightened the bone and put pins in it. The pins were attached to a round, metal frame—called a fixator—on the outside of Floyd's leg to hold the bone in place while it healed.

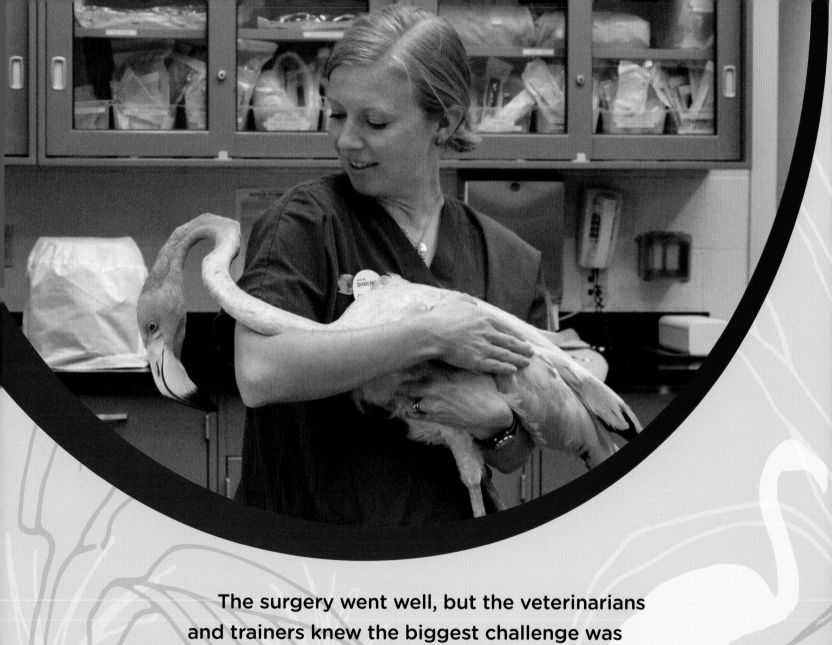

The surgery went well, but the veterinarians and trainers knew the biggest challenge was still ahead: Floyd's recovery would take even longer this time. Keeping Floyd's spirits up was important because his leg would be very sore. He would also be away from the flamingo flock for many more weeks!

To help Floyd feel more at home in the Zoo hospital, the trainers added potted plants, his favorite feeding dish, and a mirror to his recovery room. The mirror made it look like there was more than one flamingo in the room, so he wouldn't be lonely.

# Caring for Floyd

Floyd's devoted trainers did whatever it took to help him heal. For the first week and a half, they cared for him around the clock. Floyd was most comfortable when he wasn't standing on either leg, so the trainers held him on their laps at all times. They knew that Floyd was special because none of the other flamingos in the Zoo wanted to be held like that.

The trainers were surprised to learn that Floyd snored and dreamed while he slept! His snores sounded like soft honks. When he was dreaming, his eyes and legs twitched!

Floyd was wrapped in a yellow towel to keep him warm and to keep the trainers' uniforms clean. He tucked his beak under his trainer's arm to feel secure, just like he would tuck his beak under his wing if he were standing on his own.

Everyone who met Floyd grew attached to him and wanted to help him get better. Whenever Floyd's bandage was changed, the trainers and the veterinary staff decorated the new one with a different design.

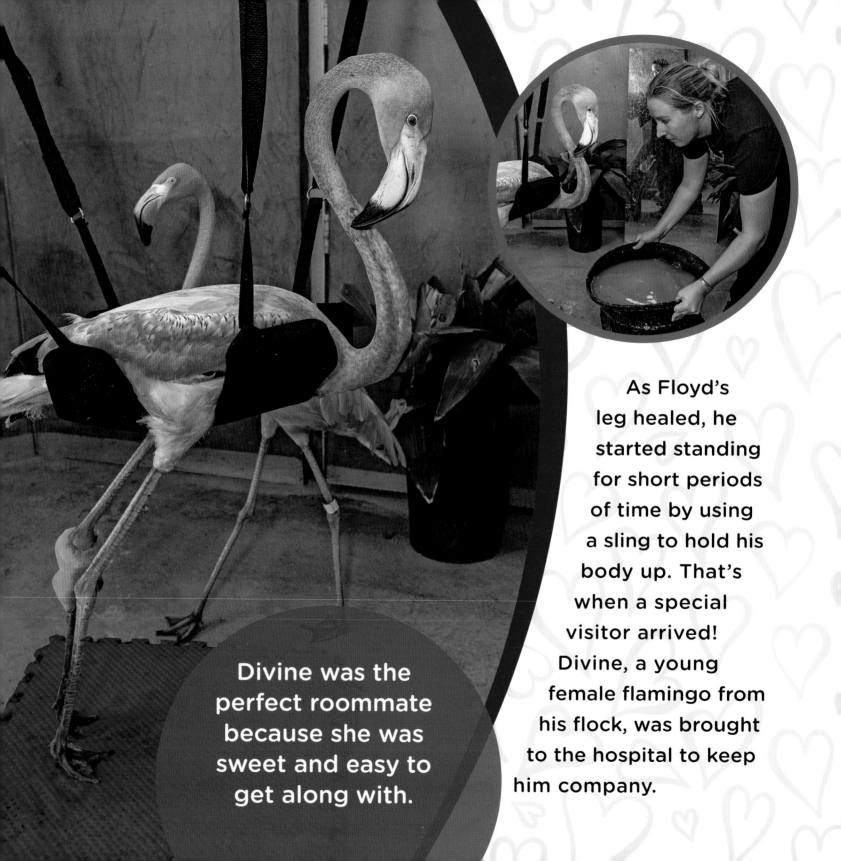

Divine was the perfect roommate because she was sweet and easy to get along with.

As Floyd's leg healed, he started standing for short periods of time by using a sling to hold his body up. That's when a special visitor arrived! Divine, a young female flamingo from his flock, was brought to the hospital to keep him company.

Even though Floyd's recovery was challenging, the trainers could tell that he wanted to get better. He made progress every day, standing for longer and longer periods of time without being held by them or supported by the sling.

# Back to the Flock

The day Floyd took his first few steps on his own, the trainers cried because they were so happy and relieved. No one had been sure he would ever walk again.

Before Floyd could be reunited with the flamingo flock, he had to walk on his own all the time. He needed good balance, too. The trainers didn't want him knocked over by the other flamingos, who could be a bit pushy.

Floyd started visiting his flamingo flock several hours a day. At first, he watched them from over a fence. He also practiced walking in a grassy area near their lagoon.

Each day, Floyd's leg grew stronger and stronger.

Finally, a month after Floyd's second surgery, his left leg was strong enough for him to rejoin his flamingo friends once more. Floyd had been through a lot, yet he never gave up his fight to get better.

FLOYD

When Floyd was reunited with the other flamingos, he strolled over to them, flapped his wings, and honked. Floyd was home again, ready to take on his job as an animal ambassador. As the friendliest flamingo in the flock, fabulous Floyd soon became one of the most popular animals in the entire San Diego Zoo! He continues to greet people today and still likes a snuggle from his trainers every once in a while.

Flamingos lay one egg at a time on a nest made of mud. Both parents take care of the egg and chick when it's hatched.

# Fun Facts about Flamingos

Flamingos are social birds. They live in flocks of varying sizes, from a few pairs to thousands of birds in one colony!

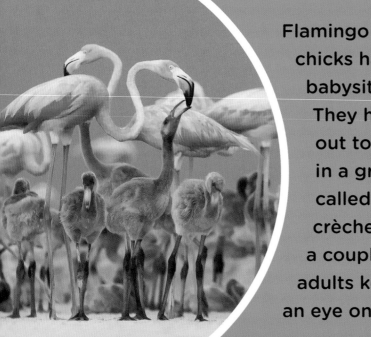

Flamingo chicks have babysitters! They hang out together in a group called a crèche while a couple of adults keep an eye on them.

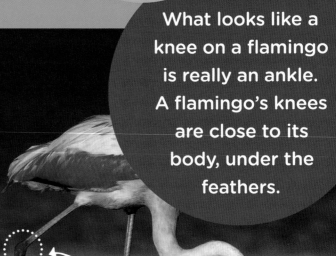

What looks like a knee on a flamingo is really an ankle. A flamingo's knees are close to its body, under the feathers.

ANKLES

Flamingos communicate with each other by making many sounds, including honking, growling, and grunting. Parents recognize their chick's "voice."

When flamingos fly, they run a few steps on the ground or water to gain speed before they take off into the air.

Flamingos' pink color comes from pigments in the foods they eat—including shrimp, mollusks, fish, insects, and flies.

Flamingos feed with their bills upside-down. They tip their heads into the water and filter feed, straining their food from the water using their beaks.

No one knows exactly how long flamingos live in the wild. They can live up to 60 years in zoos and wildlife parks.

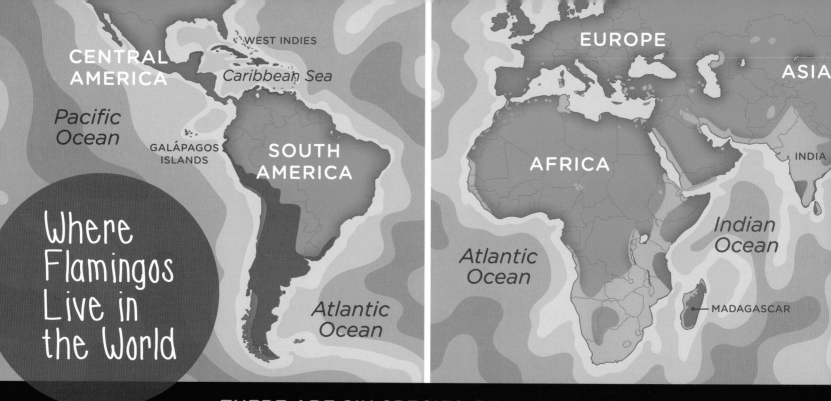

CENTRAL AMERICA

WEST INDIES

Caribbean Sea

Pacific Ocean

GALÁPAGOS ISLANDS

SOUTH AMERICA

Atlantic Ocean

EUROPE

ASIA

AFRICA

INDIA

Atlantic Ocean

Indian Ocean

MADAGASCAR

# Where Flamingos Live in the World

**THERE ARE SIX SPECIES OF FLAMINGOS: FOUR FROM THE AMERICAS AND TWO FROM AFRICA, ASIA, AND EUROPE.**

Although flamingos aren't endangered, a few species are threatened.

## Threats to Flamingos:

- Habitat loss
- Predators such as big cats, vultures, and foxes
- Poaching for feathers and eggs
- People disturbing their colonies, which causes eggs and chicks to be abandoned

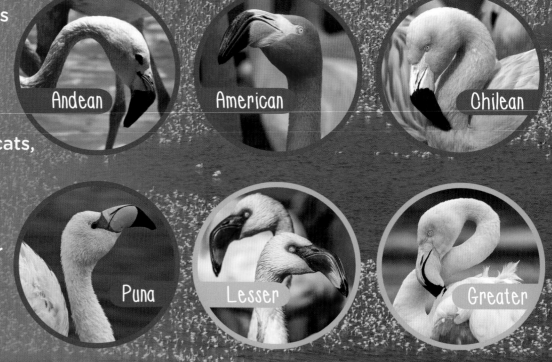

Andean

American

Chilean

Puna

Lesser

Greater